HUE COLORING

Narwhal Coloring Book

An Adult Coloring Book

Copyright © 2018 Hue Coloring
All rights reserved.

No part of this publication may be copied, reproduced in any format, by any means, electronic or otherwise, without prior consent from the copyright owner and publisher of this book.

IN THIS COLORING BOOK...
50 Beautiful Narwhal Coloring designs are included in this adult coloring book to help you relax and make your life more colorful. These illustrations are created for you to bring enjoyment to your life, and designed with beautiful patterns that appeal to adult eyes.

TIPS TO A FUN COLORING
Find a quiet space. It's easier to focus on what you are doing when there are no distractions.

Organize your materials. Lay out your coloring book and crayons, pens, or pencils.

Set the mood. Turn on some tranquil music, diffuse lavender or another relaxing oil, and make sure you have your preferred drink at hand.

Select your picture. Which image speaks to you today? That's the one you should color. Choose your palette. Select the colors you will be using for your image.

Begin coloring. This is the fun part. Don't worry about getting everything perfect; just start. If you feel you don't want to do it anymore, just stop!

SHOW US YOUR CREATION!
We'd love to hear from you, show us what you created.
Facebook: www.facebook.com/huecoloring
Pinterest: www.pinterest.com/huecoloring
Please be sure to subscribe to our newsletter by visiting: huecoloring.com. We'll show you our latest coloring projects as well as giving you information of the best deals.

Shutterstock Author: Credit Images - OlichO, Catherine Glazkova, balabolka, Toporovska Nataliia, Azuzi, Natalija Davydova, Davdeka, Dualororua, maljuk, karakotsya, sliplee, Irina Markova, Nearbirds, Isabelle Kuehn, Lotus_studio, Makhnach_S, Val_Iva, Romolo Tavani, Peter Leahy, Framework Wonderland, John A. Anderson, Rolf E. Staerk, Fer Gregory, Tharapong Talubnak